Best Mom

by Lisa Boggs
illustrated by Kersti Frigell

Core Decodable 37

Mc Graw Hill Education

Bothell, WA • Chicago, IL • Columbus, OH • New York, NY

MHEonline.com

Send all inquiries to:
McGraw-Hill Education
8787 Orion Place
Columbus, OH 43240

ISBN: 978-0-02-145825-7
MHID: 0-02-145825-1

Printed in Canada.

9 10 11 12 KOD 24

Tom slipped.
Mom helped him up.

Pam spilled it.
Mom mopped it.

Mom patted Pam.

Pam napped.

Tom acted.

Mom clapped.

Dad landed.

Mom picked him up.

Dad handed Tom a pin.
Tom pinned it on Mom.
The pin said BEST MOM.